Date Due	

The Berlin Airlift

by Michael Burgan

Content Adviser: Knox Bishop,
Former Curator, Frontiers of Flight Museum,
Dallas, Texas

Reading Adviser: Katie Van Sluys, Ph.D.,
School of Education, DePaul University

COMPASS POINT BOOKS
MINNEAPOLIS, MINNESOTA

Compass Point Books
3109 West 50th Street, #115
Minneapolis, MN 55410

Visit Compass Point Books on the Internet at *www.compasspointbooks.com*
or e-mail your request to *custserv@compasspointbooks.com*

On the cover: A C-47 cargo plane approaches Templehof Airport with food and other supplies in 1948 during the Berlin Airlift.

Photographs ©: Walter Sanders/*Life* Magazine/Time & Life Pictures/Getty Images, cover; Prints Old & Rare, back cover (far left); Library of Congress, back cover, 7, 18, 20, 21, 29; Charles Fenno Jacobs/Hulton Archive/Getty Images, 4; Hank Walker/Time & Life Pictures/Getty Images, 6, 27; J. R. Eyerman/Time & Life Pictures/Getty Images, 8; Fred Ramage/Keystone Features/Getty Images, 9; U.S. Army/Naval Historical Foundation, 11; Walter Sanders/Time & Life Pictures/Getty Images, 13; Harry S. Truman Library & Museum, 14, 15; Bettmann/Corbis, 17, 24, 26, 32, 34, 36, 37, 38, 39, 41; James Whitmore/Time Life Pictures/Getty Images, 19; Hulton-Deutsch Collection/Corbis, 22, 35; Keystone/ Getty Images, 23; Time Magazine/Time & Life Pictures/Getty Images, 31.

Managing Editor: Catherine Neitge
Page Production: Noumenon Creative
Photo Researcher: Svetlana Zhurkin
Cartographer: XNR Productions, Inc.
Library Consultant: Kathleen Baxter

Creative Director: Keith Griffin
Editorial Director: Carol Jones

Library of Congress Cataloging-in-Publication Data
Burgan, Michael.
  The Berlin Airlift/ by Michael Burgan
      p. cm.—(We the people)
  Includes bibliographical references and index.
  ISBN-13: 978-0-7565-2024-3 (hardcover)
  ISBN-10: 0-7565-2024-X (hardcover)
  ISBN-13: 978-0-7565-2426-5 (paperback)
  ISBN-10: 0-7565-2426-1 (paperback)
  1. Berlin (Germany)—History—Blockade, 1948–1949—Juvenile literature. I. Title. II. We the People (Series) (Compass Point Books)
  DD881.B799 2007
  943'.1550874—dc22   2006006766

TABLE OF CONTENTS

KEEPING A CITY ALIVE

Day after day in 1948 and 1949, the people of Berlin, Germany, looked up to the skies. Overhead, an endless stream of British and U.S. planes flew into their divided city. They brought in tons of food, gas, coal, and whatever else Berliners needed to survive. In June 1948, the Soviets had blockaded Berlin, shutting down all train, boat, and

Berlin children climbed a tree to watch a U.S. cargo plane arrive with supplies.

truck traffic into the western sectors of the city. The only thing that kept the citizens of Berlin from starving were the supplies brought in by the planes that flew around the clock.

The Berlin blockade was the result of growing tensions in the divided city of Berlin. France, Great Britain, the United States, and the Soviet Union each controlled one sector of the city. Not only was the city of Berlin divided, but so, too, was Germany itself. The country was also divided among the four nations. Those countries had worked together to defeat Germany in World War II, which ended in 1945. But now, three years later, they disagreed on how the conquered country should be ruled.

France, Great Britain, and the United States had democratic governments. These three countries were called the Western Allies. They wanted to create a democratic country out of the three zones of Germany they controlled. The Soviet Union, led by Joseph Stalin, opposed this. Stalin supported communism, a political system in which the government owns all the businesses, there is no private

5

The British sector was one of four in the divided city of Berlin.

property, and personal freedoms are often limited. Stalin
wanted a communist government in Germany that would
be friendly with the Soviet Union. He opposed creating a
democratic nation in Allied-controlled western Germany.

Stalin wanted to force the Western Allies out of
Berlin, a city deep in the Soviet zone. The Soviets controlled
the roads and railways into the city. On June 23, 1948,
Stalin ordered a blockade of the three western sectors in

Berlin under Allied control. Trains, boats, and trucks could no longer travel in and out of West Berlin. Slowly, Stalin hoped, the citizens there would run out of food and other crucial supplies. Then the U.S., British, and French leaders would either have to change the policies in Germany that Stalin disliked or leave altogether. Otherwise, the blockade would continue.

But Stalin misjudged the Allies. He thought they could never bring in enough supplies by plane. The Allies, however, began a massive airlift. During this Berlin Airlift, British and U.S. planes flew day and night into the city. They brought in the food and supplies that West Berliners needed to live. By the spring of 1949, Stalin realized his plan had failed. The Allies were not

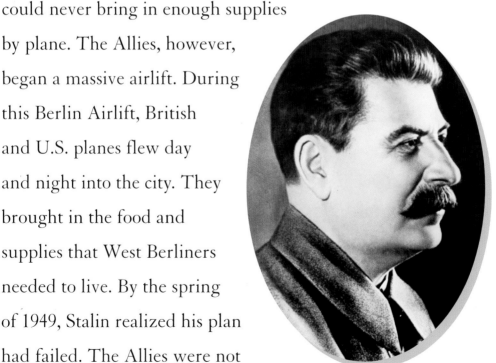

Joseph Stalin (1878–1953)

U.S. Air Force pilots stood at attention in front of the C-47 and C-54
cargo planes they flew during the Berlin Airlift.

going to leave West Berlin. Stalin ended the blockade.

The Berlin Airlift gave the Allies their first major victory in the Cold War. This struggle—not a conflict, but largely a battle of words and ideas—was between the United States and the Soviet Union, and it lasted more than 40 years. These two nations competed with each other to influence other countries around the world. The United States wanted to promote democracy, while the Soviets hoped to spread communism. By the end of 1991, though, the communist government in the Soviet Union had crumbled.

WHAT TO DO WITH GERMANY

The roots of the Berlin Airlift went back to the end of World War II. Germany had started the war by invading Poland in 1939. Eventually, the war spread across Europe, parts of Africa, and Asia, where Japan had invaded China two years earlier. On May 7, 1945, Germany surrendered, ending the war in Europe. The war ended completely a

Berlin was in ruins at the end of World War II.

few months later with the surrender of Japan.

Berlin, the German capital, had once been a beautiful city. At the war's end, however, it was filled with rubble. British and American planes had bombed the city almost daily during the last year of the war. On the ground, the Soviet army had bombarded it with its large guns. When the fighting finally stopped, the Soviets controlled the city.

In July 1945, U.S. President Harry Truman met with the leaders of the Soviet Union and Great Britain in Potsdam, Germany. At the meeting, the leaders of the so-called Big Three nations decided how to govern the defeated Germany. They agreed to split the nation into four zones. France received the fourth, though it had played a smaller role in defeating Germany. It would also play a less impor-tant role in the events that followed. The United States was clearly the most powerful of the democratic nations, with the largest military and greatest wealth.

During the war, Germany had invaded the Soviet Union. That was not the first time Germany had done

Leaders of the Big Three nations, Clement Attlee (left), Harry Truman, and Joseph Stalin, met in Potsdam to discuss Germany's future.

this. Years earlier, during World War I, it had also invaded Russia, the major part of the Soviet Union. Now Stalin wanted to make sure Germany would never invade his country again. One way to do this was to create friendly communist governments in Germany and other parts of Eastern Europe. Soviet troops controlled most of Eastern Europe, so the British and Americans could not easily stop Stalin's plans. But Germany was divided, with the Soviets in the east and the Allies in the west. Truman and British leader Clement Attlee wanted to keep democratic influence in western Germany, if not the whole country.

Although the United States and the Soviet Union had worked together to defeat Germany during the war, they never trusted each other. The Soviets opposed capitalism, the major economic system in the United States and Europe. Under capitalism, people are free to form companies and own as much property as they can afford. Americans knew that the Soviets hoped to one day destroy capitalism and spread communism.

Truman in particular grew to distrust Stalin. During the next several years, Truman tried to stop Soviet attempts to spread communism. Truman's effort was at the heart of the Cold War. The United States wanted to limit the number of countries the Soviets controlled or influenced. Truman and the Allies were dismayed by the Soviet takeover of Eastern European countries and the subjugation of the citizens. At the same time, U.S. leaders supported

Pro-communist troops paraded through Prague, Czechoslovakia, in 1948 in a show of force.

existing democratic governments. They also tried to create
new democracies where they did not exist. Both the Soviets
and Americans sent money and weapons to groups that
shared their views. The Soviets also sent military forces
to strengthen their control. Each side tried to weaken the
other's efforts to gain influence around the world.

REBUILDING EUROPE

In March 1947, President Truman announced what was called the Truman Doctrine. The United States would "support free peoples who are resisting attempted [control] by armed minorities or by outside pressures." Truman was referring to Soviet efforts to spread communism in Greece, Turkey, and Eastern Europe.

Later in the spring, Truman's advisers called for a plan to rebuild Western Europe, including Germany. Most of Europe was still suffering from the effects of the war, and the nations' economies were weak. Western Europe needed healthy economies to stay democratic. Communist systems often appealed

President Harry Truman

The Marshall Plan provided desperately needed help to war-torn Europe.

to people who were poor, since the governments promised
to keep prices low and give everyone jobs. To help Europe
rebuild, Truman wanted to give the countries aid. That aid
program was later called the Marshall Plan. It was named
for George C. Marshall, Army chief of staff during World
War II and Truman's secretary of state. Marshall was the
major creator and organizer of the relief effort.

In the Soviet Union, leaders worried about U.S. plans for Europe. Stalin did not want to lose the influence he had already gained. He also wanted Germany to be reunited at some point and to come under Soviet control. The Americans preferred that Germany be reunited, too. But Truman did not want to see Germany run by communists. As Secretary of State Marshall wrote, the United States "would regard such an [event] as the greatest threat to security of all Western Nations, including the U.S."

Fears of the Soviets' plans increased in February 1948. That month, communists in Czechoslovakia took over the country's government. Stalin had supported this move. At the same time, U.S. and Western European officials secretly met in London to discuss the future of Germany. The events in Czechoslovakia helped convince them to take quick action. They agreed that the British, American, and French zones should be combined into one country, West Germany.

Stalin had spies at the London meeting, and he soon

learned about the plan. He came up with his own plan to try to stop the creation of West Germany. In March, he said to German communists in the Soviet zone, "Let's make a joint effort. Perhaps we can kick [the Allies] out."

Berliners read the newspapers to learn about Allied plans to form West Germany.

17

Atomic bombs like those dropped on Japan could kill tens of thousands of people.

Stalin did not want to fight the Allies. He knew the Americans had bombs that used the immense power stored inside some atoms. The United States had dropped two of these atomic bombs on Japan at the end of World War II. But Stalin thought he could hurt the Allies in a soft spot—Berlin. Since his troops controlled the territory around the city, they could prevent trains, trucks, and ships from entering it. A blockade of Berlin might slow or stop the efforts to create West Germany.

THE "LITTLE LIFT"

On March 30, 1948, Soviet military officials in Berlin sent a message to Allied leaders. Starting April 1, the Soviets claimed the right to inspect all trains, trucks, and boats entering Berlin. They would turn back any cargo that they did not want entering the city.

General Lucius Clay was the military governor of the U.S. zone in Germany. He saw the Russian plan "as the first of a series of ... measures designed to drive us from Berlin." He responded angrily. Clay told U.S. officials he wanted U.S. soldiers "to open fire if Soviet soldiers attempt to enter our trains." But like Stalin,

General Lucius Clay

19

President Truman did not want a war. He and his advisers told Clay not to fire on Soviet troops.

Clay and the British then decided they simply would not send any military trains into Berlin. Instead, they began to supply their troops by air. Clay asked General Curtis LeMay to handle the American effort. The planes flew along paths that the Soviets had earlier said the Allies could use. LeMay's men flew C-47 Skytrain cargo planes, which the pilots affectionately called Gooney Birds, and brought in tons of food for the U.S. troops. These efforts were later called the Little Lift.

During this time, most civilian traffic still flowed in and out of Berlin. Passenger trains freely entered

General Curtis LeMay

U.S. soldiers checked traffic to and from Potsdam in response to Soviet restrictions.

the city. Allied soldiers and citizens were able to drive into the city, but German citizens were sometimes stopped. The Soviets did not call their early efforts to limit travel a "blockade." They claimed they were looking for criminals or other "shady individuals." To the Americans, the Soviets said the restrictions were the result of "technical difficulties." But within Berlin, civilians and Allied officials knew the Soviets wanted to disrupt life in the city. And they wondered what Stalin would do next.

The Little Lift continued through the spring. During

21

A U.S. soldier guarded a shipment of coal on its way to Berlin.

this time, the Americans also began bringing coal into the
city, trying to create a stockpile. The coal was used to heat
homes and stoves. The stockpile would help keep Germans
warm that winter if Berlin faced a complete blockade. To
the Soviets, however, the Little Lift seemed a failure. A
report from April 17 said, "Clay's attempts to create 'an airlift' connecting Berlin with the Western zones have proved
[useless]." The Soviets had confidence they could further
weaken the Allies in Berlin.

THE AIRLIFT BEGINS

For several months, the Soviets added new restrictions on travel. They limited how many passenger trains could enter the city and how many boats could bring in cargo. Then in June, relations between the two sides worsened.

The Allies introduced new currency—the deutsche mark—in West Germany. They knew that a stable currency had to be in place if the German economy were to recover. The Soviets said the new money could not be used in Berlin. Instead, they printed their own new currency for the city. Residents, however, could buy more goods with

A German rushed through Berlin with a newspaper announcing the new deutsche mark.

23

the Allies' currency, so they ignored the Soviet money.

The Soviets were angry with the Allies for releasing the new currency without their approval. They encouraged communists in eastern Berlin to lead riots, which turned bloody. In the western sectors, however, most people supported the Allies and their currency. On June 24, 1948, Berlin's mayor, Ernst Reuter, spoke to a crowd of 70,000 Berliners.

German political leaders spoke to a huge crowd on June 24, 1948, asking for the world's help in combating Soviet aggression.

He told them that the real issue was not currency, but the future of Berlin. He hoped the whole world would help the city "in the decisive phase of the fight for freedom."

The same day, the Soviets began their full blockade of Berlin. They prevented trains, trucks, and boats from bringing in the 12,000 tons (10,800 metric tons) of supplies the city used each day. They also cut off electricity to the western sectors. The plants that supplied the power there were located in the Soviet sector. The citizens in the west— about 2.3 million people—had enough food to last about a month and enough coal for 45 days.

General Clay called the blockade "one of the most ruthless efforts in modern times to use mass starvation for political [force]." He wanted to break the blockade with armed trucks, but President Truman rejected that idea. Once again, he did not want to risk a war. If Berlin were going to survive, its goods would have to come by plane. Truman accepted an idea first suggested by the British. He ordered a huge airlift of supplies.

A U.S. Army armored car patrolled the streets of Berlin at the start of the blockade.

In Berlin, Clay began the airlift even before receiving approval from U.S. officials. He met with Mayor Reuter and explained the plan. The general told Reuter that it would take time to get enough planes in place. Berliners might have to cut back on their food. Clay worried that the people might grumble or lose faith in the Allies. Reuter told him that the Berliners would be fine—just bring in what you can. Clay then met with General LeMay. "General, we're going to haul coal into Berlin," Clay said. "We're going to keep this city alive."

Officially, the Berlin Airlift began on June 26. The American part of the airlift was called Operation Vittles, while the British called their efforts Operation Plain Fare. The airlift was often referred to as "LeMay's Coal and Feed Company." The first C-47s landed at Tempelhof and Gatow airports, carrying 200 tons (180 metric

Mayor Ernst Reuter

tons) of flour. They were soon joined by C-54 Skymasters, larger transport planes that could carry up to 10 tons (9 metric tons) per trip. Radio operators nicknamed any C-54 flying west "Big Willie." Flying east, a C-54 was called "Big Easy."

Meanwhile, Clay ordered his own blockade of certain supplies into East Berlin. Even with the two blockades in place, some goods went back and forth between East and

The air corridors leading to Berlin were each 20 miles (32 km) wide.

West Berlin. And the Soviets allowed West Berliners to come east to buy food. Most residents, however, refused the offer. They would rather suffer than deal with the communists.

After the first few months of the airlift, the Allies

U.S. Air Force C-47 transport planes waited in line to be unloaded at night in Berlin.

were delivering several thousand tons of supplies every day. This included medicine and paper for printing. But coal and food were the most important items.

Meanwhile, the Allies and the Soviets held talks through the summer, hoping to end the crisis. Neither side, however, would back down. The Soviets would not even admit that a blockade was in place. In public, they referred to the situation as the "so-called Berlin crisis."

LIFE UNDER THE BLOCKADE

The blockade and airlift sometimes created dangers. Some planes crashed during bad weather, killing their pilots and crews. The use of a new kind of radar helped limit these accidents, but 79 soldiers and civilians lost their lives during the heroic effort to save Berlin.

At times, Soviet fighter planes annoyed the cargo planes filling Berlin's skies. The Soviet planes flew close to the Allied aircraft, then quickly pulled away. They hoped to frighten the Allied pilots. The Soviets also used electronic jamming devices to interfere with navigation and launched weather balloons directly into the planes' paths. But the Soviets would never shoot at the planes. As always, Stalin did not want to risk a war.

President Truman was determined not to pull out of Germany or change his policies. He gave Clay and LeMay even more planes, which flew in from all over the world. Still, no one knew how long the airlift would last.

Planes landed day and night, and the military hired civilians to help unload them. As the crews learned their jobs, they could unload 9 tons (8 metric tons) of coal in just seven minutes. Then, as one empty plane took off, another loaded plane took its place. All together, the Americans and British, with some

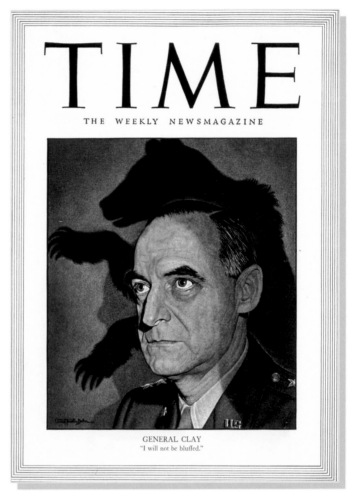

TIME

THE WEEKLY NEWSMAGAZINE

GENERAL CLAY
"I will not be bluffed."

The Russian bear, representing the Soviet Union, loomed behind General Lucius Clay on a 1948 Time *magazine cover.*

help from the French, brought more than 2.3 million tons (2 million metric tons) of food and supplies into West Berlin.

Even with the food and supplies that arrived, life was

A hairstylist curled a customer's hair outside because there was no electricity in her Berlin shop.

hard in West Berlin. People had to use as little coal as possible, so they were often cold. Electricity was available for just four hours a day. And food was rationed, meaning few ate as much as they would like. But they did eat balanced, although meager, meals and received vitamin pills from the Allies.

The local communists also tried to stir up trouble. In September, the city's government met in East Berlin. The communists used violence to break up the meeting. A few days later, Mayor Reuter called for Berliners to meet to protest the communists' actions and show support for the airlift. About 300,000 people crammed into a public square to hear Reuter speak. He said, "People of America, England, France ... you cannot abandon this city and its people."

One U.S. pilot tried to cheer up the children of Berlin. Lieutenant Gail Halvorsen made tiny parachutes out of handkerchiefs and tied them to chocolate bars and other candies. He then flew low over the city. Halvorsen slightly wiggled the wings of his plane. This told the children he was about to drop his load of candy. They then scrambled to catch the little parachutes. Soon, the children were writing letters to the U.S. base to thank him and ask for more. They called Halvorsen "Uncle Wiggly Wings"

33

When the weather was too bad to drop candy from an airplane,
Lieutenant Gail Halvorsen handed out treats on the ground.

and the "Chocolate Flyer." He was also known as the "Candy Bomber." The German children, however, knew that food was not the only thing they needed from the Americans. One child told Halvorsen, "Just don't give up on us when the weather gets bad. But we can get along without enough to eat. Some day we'll have enough. But if we lose our freedom we may never get it back."

INTO THE NEW YEAR

In October, President Truman provided more planes for the airlift. General Clay said, "The airlift will be continued until the blockade is lifted." Clay also told the president that the airlift was boosting spirits in Berlin. More people were eagerly trying to rebuild their city. More were rejecting communism.

With the arrival of the new planes, the airlift was able

A line of C-47 Skytrains had their cargoes unloaded at a Berlin airport.

35

to bring in 5,000 tons (4,500 metric tons) of supplies every day. But British officials were still not sure that would be enough. The demand for coal would rise during the winter. And the weather would worsen, making it harder for pilots to land. In November, fog often clung to the airfields. The daily tonnage shipped fell to less than 3,800 tons (3,420 metric tons). This was less than what Berliners needed to survive. But by the end of the month, more planes arrived,

German laborers, mostly women, helped build a new airfield in Berlin.

A Berlin woman scraped bark from a tree to use to start a cooking fire.

and a new airport opened. Tegel Airfield was built in just 49 days by Army engineers and Berlin volunteers.

Coal, however, was still in short supply, and most of it went to Berlin's factories. Some people began chopping down the city's trees to use as firewood.

Despite the difficulties, more supplies arrived each month. On April 16, 1949—Easter Sunday—the U.S. pilots and crew set a record for the airlift. They delivered almost 13,000 tons (11,700 metric tons) of supplies in just one day. It meant that a C-54 landed every minute for 24 straight

Police in the Soviet zone searched a man's cart as he traveled between sectors.

hours. The Americans called this their Easter Parade.

After that record was set, the Allies worked harder than ever. They increased the daily average to almost 9,000 tons (8,100 metric tons).

Meanwhile, Clay's blockade was having an effect. People in the Soviet zone were not getting coal and materials needed to run their factories. The Allies had shut down the supply of chemicals, steel, and other goods going into the East. And goods produced in eastern Germany could not be shipped west through Berlin, as they had in the past. The economy in the East began to weaken.

END OF THE BLOCKADE

Stalin saw the problems that the Allies' blockade caused in the Soviet zone. He also saw that the Allies were moving forward with their plans to create the nation of West Germany. In addition, the Allies had formed a new military organization since the blockade started. The United States

The airlift to save Berlin was the first major action of the U.S. Air Force, which was founded in 1947.

39

had led this effort to unite the democratic countries of North America and Western Europe. The North Atlantic Treaty Organization (NATO) was born in April 1949.

With the Allies gaining a firm grip in Western Europe, Stalin was ready to end the blockade. Talks between the Allies and the Soviets, which had been ongoing through the winter, led to the announcement on May 12, 1949, that both blockades would end. The Allies did not meet any of the Soviets' earlier demands. The new currency was still used in Berlin, and the three Allied zones in Germany would become a democratic German nation. Stalin had gained nothing with his blockade.

On the night of May 11, the Soviets turned on the electricity in West Berlin. Just after midnight, the first cars and trucks began to enter the city. The airlift, however, did not end right away. It took several months for the city to build up its supply of food and coal. Allied planes continued to fly in goods until the end of September. Then the airlift was officially over.

The children of Berlin knew that the airlift meant their survival and their freedom.

The Berlin Airlift was just one of many battles in the Cold War. As with some others, no weapons were actually fired. But the Allies knew they needed all their military skills and courage just as they would during a traditional war. The airlift, according to President Truman, "had become a symbol of America's ... dedication to the cause of freedom."

41

GLOSSARY

blockade—a military effort to keep goods from entering and leaving a region

capitalism—an economic system that allows people to freely create businesses and own as much property as they can afford

civilian—a person who is not in the military

communism—a system in which goods and property are owned by the government and shared in common

currency—paper bills and coins used as money

economic—relating to the way a country runs its industry, trade, or finance

secretary of state—the head of the U.S. State Department and the president's leading adviser in dealing with other countries

sector—an area or portion

stockpile—a large collection of goods saved for future use during a shortage

subjugation—an act of bringing under control and into submission

42

DID YOU KNOW?

- For a time, German workers unloading planes stole shoes brought into Berlin. The Allies ended this by bringing in left-footed and right-footed shoes on separate flights.

- General William H. Tunner (1906–1983) has been called the genius behind the Berlin Airlift. During World War II, he had organized an airlift of supplies over the "hump" of the Himalayas and into China. He coordinated the flights into and out of Berlin with great success. He later coordinated an airlift during the Korean War.

- The British army and navy provided specialized aircraft for the airlift. The Short Sunderland flying boats flew salt into the city, landing on Lake Havel in downtown Berlin. Specialized fuel tanker versions of the Halifax bombers carried most of the oil, gasoline, and fuel into the city. American and British commercial airlines flew during the airlift, as well.

- General Lucius Clay, who died in 1978, is buried at the U.S. Military Academy at West Point, New York. At his grave is a memorial from the citizens of Berlin. It says in German, *"Wir danken dem Bewahrer unserer Freiheit"*—"We thank the defender of our freedom."

IMPORTANT DATES

Timeline

1945
In May, World War II ends in Europe; in July, Great Britain, the United States, France, and the Soviet Union each take control of one part of Germany and the city of Berlin.

1947
In March, President Truman outlines U.S. desires to limit the spread of communism; in June, the Marshall Plan is announced.

1948
In April, the Little Lift begins in Berlin; in June, the Soviet Union places a full blockade around Berlin, leading to the Berlin Airlift.

1949
In April, the United States and 10 other nations form NATO; in May, the Soviet blockade ends; in September, the Berlin Airlift ends.

IMPORTANT PEOPLE

LUCIUS CLAY (1897–1978)
U.S. military governor and commander of U.S. troops in Europe from 1947 to 1949, when he retired; Clay served as President John F. Kennedy's personal representative in Berlin in 1961 and 1962

CURTIS LEMAY (1906–1990)
U.S. general who commanded the Air Force in Europe and was in charge of the Berlin Airlift; he later served as Air Force chief of staff from 1961 to 1965

GEORGE C. MARSHALL (1880–1959)
U.S. general who served as Army chief of staff during World War II and as President Truman's secretary of state; he won the Nobel Peace Prize in 1953 for his work to promote economic recovery in Europe

ERNST REUTER (1889–1953)
Longtime politician and mayor of West Berlin from 1948 until his death of a heart attack; he traveled to the United States several times during the Berlin blockade to rally support and raise awareness

HARRY S. TRUMAN (1884–1972)
Thirty-third president of the United States; he became president when Franklin Delano Roosevelt died in 1945

WANT TO KNOW MORE?

At the Library

Brager, Bruce L. *The Iron Curtain: The Cold War in Europe*. Philadelphia: Chelsea House, 2004.

Cannarella, Deborah. *Harry S. Truman*. Minneapolis: Compass Point Books, 2003.

Downing, David. *Joseph Stalin*. Chicago: Heinemann Library, 2002.

Irwin, David W., Jr. *Highway to Freedom: The Berlin Airlift*. Paducah, Ky.: Turner Publishing Company, 2002.

Provan, John, and R.E.G. Davies. *Berlin Airlift: The Effort and the Aircraft*. McLean, Va.: Paladwr Press, 1998.

Sirimarco, Elizabeth. *The Cold War*. New York: Benchmark Books, 2005.

On the Web

For more information on the *Berlin Airlift*, use FactHound

to track down Web sites related to this book.

1. Go to *www.facthound.com*

2. Type in this book ID: 075652024X

3. Click on the *Fetch It* button.

Your trusty FactHound will fetch the best Web sites for you!

On the Road

Harry S. Truman Library & Museum

500 W. U.S. Highway 24

Independence, MO 64050

800/833-1225

Information about Harry Truman
and his role during the Cold War

George C. Marshall Museum

Virginia Military Institute Parade

Lexington, VA 24450

540/463-7103

A museum dedicated to General
Marshall and his military and
diplomatic roles

Look for more We the People books about this era:

The 19th Amendment
ISBN 0-7565-1260-3

The Dust Bowl
ISBN 0-7565-0837-1

Ellis Island
ISBN 0-7565-0302-7

The Great Depression
ISBN 0-7565-0152-0

The Korean War
ISBN 0-7565-2027-4

Navajo Code Talkers
ISBN 0-7565-0611-5

Pearl Harbor
ISBN 0-7565-0680-8

The Persian Gulf War
ISBN 0-7565-0612-3

September 11
ISBN 0-7565-2029-0

The Sinking of the USS Indianapolis
ISBN 0-7565-2031-2

The Statue of Liberty
ISBN 0-7565-0100-8

The Titanic
ISBN 0-7565-0614-X

The Tuskegee Airmen
ISBN 0-7565-0683-2

The Vietnam Veterans Memorial
ISBN 0-7565-2032-0

A complete list of We the People titles is available on our Web site:
www.compasspointbooks.com

INDEX

About the Author

Michael Burgan is a freelance writer of books for children and adults. A history graduate of the University of Connecticut, he has written more than 90 fiction and nonfiction children's books. For adult audiences, he has written news articles, essays, and plays. Michael Burgan is a recipient of an Educational Press Association of America award.